*DAN RIVER ANTHOLOGY, 1995*

edited by

Richard S. Danbury, III

Dan River Press

Copyright © 1995 Dan River Press, for authors included. All rights returned to authors following publication.

Welcome to the ongoing series of the *Dan River Anthology* (since 1984). *The Dan* is produced by dues and donations of members of the Conservatory of American Letters. CAL is a nonprofit, tax-exempt, literary/educational foundation.

**Dan River Press**
**PO Box 298**
**Thomaston, ME 04861**

# Contents

| | |
|---|---|
| Harold Huber | 1 |
| Carmen M. Pursifull | 6 |
| Rita Ciresi | 7/9 |
| Emily Robinson | 8/46 |
| Robert Patrick O'Sullivan | 10 |
| John Gorman | 13 |
| Ryan McLaughlin | 17/79 |
| J. F. Pytko | 18 |
| Elizabeth Marchitti | 20 |
| Don Thornton | 22 |
| William Rose | 23 |
| Desoree Thompson | 29 |
| Anneke Mason | 30 |
| John Marrs | 32 |
| Carol Ellms | 33 |
| Patricia Greenwood | 35 |
| Sherry B. Hanson | 36 |
| Marcie Leitzke | 38 |
| Kevin Lavey | 39 |
| Lu Spurlock | 43 |
| Sylvia Relation | 44 |
| Ralph Pezzullo | 45 |
| Joyce S. Mettelman | 47 |
| Kay Renz | 50 |
| Olivia Diamond | 51 |
| Renee Goldberg | 54 |
| Thomas Plante | 55 |

| | |
|---|---|
| Ginger Roberts | 56 |
| Alan C. March | 57 |
| Sol Rubin | 60 |
| Roy Schwartzman | 61 |
| Marijane G. Ricketts | 62 |
| Mary Engel | 63 |
| Irene G. Dayton | 64 |
| David Norris | 65/74 |
| Phyllis de la Garza | 66 |
| Gwendolyn Carr | 68 |
| John W. Gracy | 69 |
| James Rossignol | 76 |
| Sy Hakim | 77 |
| Richard Alan Bunch | 80 |
| Randall Brock | 81 |
| Dr. Doris M. Carter | 82 |
| Christine Swanberg | 83 |
| Ginni Noonan | 84 |
| L. K. Hoffman | 85 |

# DEDICATED TO

# LEONARD H. GINSBURG

# DAN RIVER ANTHOLOGY, 1995

*Harold Huber*
*Ottertail, MN*

## BLOOD BROTHERS

If you step on a nail, the first thing you do is pull it out. The second is you stick it through something red and hang it high above your head when you go to bed. Then you don't get blood poison. I learned that from Mr. Rags when I was six years old and he was my best friend. How I met him was I always had a stand in the back alley. A stand is a kind of store. I had my own business at the age of nine years old. I sold used comic books, used toys, used marbles and polliwogs. These are sometimes called tadpoles. I had the most customers for polliwogs, and second was comic books. I got the polliwogs at the dump a block from my house. I could find hundreds of them - usually in empty coffee cans full of water, but sometimes in parts of barrels and wagons that didn't leak. The water has to be very old and then the polliwogs will be there. Mr. Rags told me they would not turn into frogs but to mosquitoes. So I put that on my sign and sold five jars in one day. Mr. Rags was my sign-helper.

I call him Mr. Rags, but all the other people called him plain "Rags". That is because he bought your rags. He had a wooden cart painted black, and he pulled it by two poles that stuck out in front. He called, "Rags! Rags!" as he walked down the alley, and sometimes people came out and gave him their old clothes or traded him for something on his cart. This is called barter. The first time Mr. Rags met me, he bartered me two oranges with all the rotten cut off for one Captain Marvel. I call him *Mister* because it means more respectful than just Rags. His real name is Mr. Kalas, but I'm the only one he told that to. That's because we were best friends then.

One day he asked me if I wanted to go with him on his rounds. I said yes right away and did it almost every day after that. He helped me make the "Closed" sign for my stand. We always started behind the hotel where the alley is all in bricks. The back of the hotel has an iron stairs that goes right up to the top of the building, and you know you would vomit if you went up there. We called, "Rags!" over and over, but lots of times nobody had any. Then came the IGA, and we always got oranges there from the big iron box...sometimes even watermelon. He cut off the rotten parts with a long knife with a white handle and all jewels covering it. It came from the Old Country. That's where Mr. Rags came from too, and it must be *very* old because *he* is over one hundred years old. I believe him. I know it's true. They did not have electric light bulbs or even a radio there.

He always bartered me for comic books. This is what he liked to give to his son, Nikos. Nikos couldn't come ragging with his father because he was very sick and very different. I asked Mr. Rags every time how he was different, but he didn't want to tell me. He said it made his heart hurt to talk about it. So, I just saved my best comics for Nikos and stopped asking. All my comics came from the dump, and we went there every day. Anyone would be surprised to see how many good rags and comics you can find there for free at the dump. But you have to be careful when you do it. There are bums there and people that are called Hoodlums. One time Mr. Rags saved us from them by hollering loud in his language from the Old Country, and then by making his fists smoke in their faces. The Hoodlums got so scared when they saw his hands smoking, that they ran away and we were saved.

One other time at the dump, he threw me under the rags on his cart when a drunk man waved a gun at us. The drunk man was standing on top of a broken car without any doors. He was doing number-one when he saw us. He started to yell that me and Mr. Rags should repent our sins and go to Hell. He said he was sent to smite us down because we were Babylons or something like that. Mr. Rags quickly pushed me on the cart and covered me up with a white wedding dress. I heard him say the words again. Then I heard the drunk man make a croaky sound and lots of racket and then nothing. When I came out from under everything, I couldn't see the man anywhere. I even looked inside the car and under the hood. Mr. Rags laughed and mussed up my hair and told me not to ask so many questions.

My friend taught me the best tricks there are. If I wanted to be, I could be the greatest magician in the world. But I am not to do any of the tricks where other people can see me. I will be struck dead if I do. I know it's true. He said they are secret tricks and you only must do them with your blood brothers. How we are blood brothers is that he had a very big blue jewel like a diamond with a pin to stick it into your clothes. First we went to the place in the dump where the cliff-swallows make their holes. We squatted down there and Mr. Rags held the jewel tight in his fist until it got warm from the blood under his skin. When he opened his fingers, the jewel was all wet and it sparkled. He told me a word to say so the pin prick wouldn't hurt...and it didn't! Then we pressed our wrists together and the blood made us blood brothers. Now our spirits will ever be together.

I loved Mr. Rags when we were best friends. I wished he could be my father instead of my real one. Mr. Rags always patted my neck and said I was his other son. One day I patted my real father's neck. I thought it would make him like me more. But that was on a drunk day, so it didn't work. Even my mother has to be careful when he's drunk. She liked it when I patted her neck, but the trouble with my mother is you must make sure she doesn't have her nervous headaches. I think she had one the day I patted her, because she cried while she said to clean up my mess in the alley. Mr. Rags never gets mad and he thinks being drunk is the wrong thing — like that man in the dump. He doesn't believe in headaches or that messes hurt you. Some day Mr. Rags will take me to live with him is what he promised me. Then I will be very happy.

I saved a good comic for Nikos every time I had my stand. I tried to give them as a present for Nikos, but Mr. Rags said we had to barter. He usually bartered me fruit and sometimes a smashed cake with still plenty of frosting left. The best was when he bartered me new tricks, but he was nervous that I would do them for other people. I had to prick open my brother-spot to make sure he believed me that I wouldn't. It made me feel so good when he told me that Nikos loved the comics I saved for him. I thought it must be awful not to go ragging with his father, and maybe the comics made up for it.

When my birthday was coming the next day, Mr. Rags asked me what I wanted for a present. I said it was something he *could* give me, but I knew he wouldn't want to. He promised that if it was something he could give, he would do it. I made him touch blood-spots and then I told him. I said I wanted to meet Nikos. Mr. Rags didn't say anything for a very long time. He kept turning his big ring around and around on his finger. Then he patted my neck and said he would bring his son tomorrow...on my birthday.

When I got to the dump, I thought Mr. Rags broke his promise. No one was with him...only his cart full of rags. His eyes looked funny when he said Happy Birthday. When I asked him where's Nikos, he moved his head for me to follow him to the cliff-swallow place where it's very private. The cliffs are at the back of the dump where nothing good is and nobody goes. When we got there, he put his hands on my cheeks and said he didn't forget his promise. I had to stand right up between the cart handles and then he threw back a lumpy piece of cloth. All I could see was the top thing of a baby buggy like a curved roof. Mr. Rags put his arm around my shoulder and then folded the buggy roof back.

There was Nikos. He didn't have any clothes on and all around him was black velvet like when you buy a diamond ring. His skin was white like a grub worm and he didn't have any arms. He was littler than me, but his head was bigger than Mr. Rags' and he couldn't lift it off the velvet. I thought I was going to have to be sick, but I didn't so that I wouldn't hurt Mr. Rags' feelings. I held out an almost new Wonder Woman and laid it on his stomach. I told him, "This is for you, Nikos...a present on my birthday." His eyes rolled down slow until they could see the comic and then his mouth laughed. When he started to grunt, Mr. Rags said I should put my wrist on his mouth. He sucked on my arm and then started to cry. Mr. Rags pulled down the buggy roof and patted my neck. He was crying too. When a hundred year old man is crying, it makes you feel very sad. Then he pushed the cart down the alley and went home.

My father didn't like it when he found out that I went with Mr. Rags. My father said he was a black Jew and a gypsy. He hated Mr. Rags and he didn't even know him! My mother cried so hard to me that I had to cry too. When she was hugging me, that's when I thought I could trust her. I told her about the poor little boy with no arms so she would feel sorry and let me stay friends with Mr. Rags. That was the worst mistake that could ever be. She told my father and he started calling people on the telephone. I screamed at him that he should leave Mr. Rags alone. I never saw him get so mad. He made my nose bleed and locked me in my room. I hate him for what he did. I even hate my mother too. She is a Babylon.

Mr. Rags has not been in my alley since my birthday. My mother and father say I must never speak his name again, but I speak it all the time...to myself. His picture was in the papers. It said he lived in back of the caves where the IGA grows mushrooms, and that he is accused of insanity. They found Mrs. Rags there too. Mrs. T. Kalas. She was a modern Egyptian mummy. They also accuse him of murder, but Mr. Rags said nobody killed her. She just died. I believe him. I know it's true. They made him go to a place called Black Falls. The papers did not talk about Nikos at all. Even when grown-ups talk to my parents, they never say Nikos. Nobody found him there. Nobody believes he is...except me. I tried to think of how to go to the caves and find Nikos and take care of him.

My father and mother said when I start school, this nonsense will go out of my head. That's what they called him..."nonsense." It means something to laugh at! They are wrong though. Nothing is going out of my head. They won't laugh pretty soon.

At night I practice the tricks Mr. Rags taught me...I mean only the one trick. When *they* are asleep, I take off my pajamas and go to the mirror in my room. I can see it even when the lights are out. I squeeze my hands together so hard that they shake. I make my eyes go cross-eyed and stick my tongue out as far as it will go. Then I push my chin down on my neck until it feels like I will blow up. How I know I almost have it right is that last night, some blood came out on my brother-spot. As soon as I can get my hands to smoke, then I can relax. When that happens, all that is left to do is I put my hands on the mirror on each side of my face. Then the glass turns ruby red, there will be Mr. Rags! Nikos will be sitting on his shoulders and his mouth will be open and laughing again. We will change from best friends into *true* blood brothers. They will talk to me in Mr. Rags' old language and I will understand every word. He'll say that I don't ever have to go to school. He'll say that tomorrow night or the next night, he will break through the glass and take me with him and our spirits will ever be together. I believe it. I know it is true.

*Carmen M Pursifull*
*Champaign, IL*

## THE TOREADOR

        he waves his cape of dreams
        a dandy in tights
        which cup
        like a squeezed fist
        his identity
        back arched
        taunting stomping bull
        into a locked stare
        a dance macabre
        the passo doble
        hips barely moving
        from impaling death
        inviting that thrill
        of lying on train-tracks
        a bridge leap
        tempting knife's thrust
        daring psychosis
        from sleeplessness
        grabbing the horns
        straddling death
        riding it
        penetrating
        dark/damp desires
        swallowed
        by surrender
        cleopatra-clutched
        desperately crazed
        under a stoic mask

        the fear of a man

        who has fallen in love

*Rita Ciresi*
*Roanoke, VA*

# THE REBEL BRIDE

Later he said I was born boring, then grew vicious,
but let me tell you gals, it was quick as a clip of scissors
in a Biscayne beauty salon that I became one of history's
all-time bitches.

Pouring over the photos of a fashion magazine
I started thinking heroines and hairdos and wondering
why Eleanor of Acquaitaine squeezed a birdhouse on her head,
why Mary Queen of Scots braided her traitorous mane
before it fell, with a thud of the ax, over the block,
why Cleopatra cooed, *a blunt cut and bangs, and don't hold
the henna, honey.*

Was it all for Antony, for James, for Henry? For God
Joan of Arc may have shaved her head,
but high on the crest of my permanent wave
I felt not-so-blessed to hear these ungodly female voices:

*They serve a wonderful lunch.*
*I'm mad about their housewares.*
*I said I'll take that dress in a light peach, but only if you have flats to match.*
*Mousse first, brush second, and last but not least, hair spray!*
*She was in labor 35 hours.*
*She had that infection for months.*
*She made a lovely bride, a beautiful corpse.*
*I weighed 100 when I married, look at me now.*

I looked. Was it love that beheaded us in the polished mirrors,
a cute little crush that led our great teenage heroine, Anne Frank,

**(more)**

to fasten a cheap barrette in her hair?
Dazed, I came out from under the helmet of the hair dryer
to dutifully take my place on a honeymoon cruise

and sailing beneath that ominous douche bag of Miami moon
I shook out my stubborn, artificial curls and decided to conquer the world.

*

*Emily Robinson*
*Kensington, MD*

## ON MY RAFT

Often I can hear the roar
of frightening rapids, before
I get there.
Gathering courage
I can better prepare
To withstand the battering.

Other times I am relaxed
Unprepared to be taxed
Around the bend.
Every power
I possess, I spend
To reach calm waters again.

Sometimes I feel myself free-fall
Over some unseen rock-wall
I can only hope
For strength
Enough to cope
To surface, swim, survive.

*Rita Ciresi*
*Roanoke, VA*

## VARIATION ON THE THEME OF LA CI DAREM LA MANO

*Give me your hand,*
*say yes.*
*—Don Giovanni*

At 3 a.m. I shuddered as the Sandman's grip betrayed me
and Don Giovanni's aria puzzled me 'til morning.
The logistics of it, I mean. When he went for those women,
did he hold out his right hand or his left?

Was it his bug-eyed knuckles, the sly wink of his pinkie
or the sleepy droop of his thumb that won them over?
Did they even care? Dumb virgins. No memory.
Unaware that even the recollection of the first grip of passion

—tenuous, excited, shy, grabby—
can't soften the callous of *post coitum triste*.
It must have been the left hand the sleepless lyricist thought of.
Who thinks in German at 3 a.m.?

In the dark we dream in the language of love,
and *left* comes out unconscious, insidious, sinestro.

*Robert Patrick O'Sullivan*
*San Diego, CA*

## THE LAST CELLO SONG
*(for Melody)*

For years now I have been expecting it-
the announcement that the Show is indeed
finally over,
that our acts had been replaced with newer talent,
our microphones had been unplugged.

The Magicians having fled with their bright silks flying, and
those jewel-studded wands,
    their broken-wing'd white doves were now
forever desperate against Open Sky, and
the enticement of a freedom they could never have;
the Dramatists have rent the grand curtains
into tattered halves, stealing,
with all the costuming, props and backdrops
they could carry,
into a forbidding, empty night;
        turn the houselights on
        and find the impostors gone...
Even the Poets had given up any sense
of hope that there could be time left
for a last walk beneath the hallowed
opium dome
and, together with the sloe-eyed Prophets,
had necromanced into the dark hours in a feeble attempt
to concur that there would be a Sign
in the heavens first; but no Sign had come.
All were gone by dawn's light,

**(more)**

journeying across the width of the Continent in search of new Kingdoms.
>	In the Great Silence that was left behind,
>	the True Lovers ran in their blind panic
>	throughout the grounds and courtyards
>	in search of answers, in search of
>	at least one remaining person other than themselves
>	who could help them remember;
>	for they had slept soundly through the night,
>	and could not understand the meaning of this great Silence
>	suddenly imposed on them.
>	"Why are we being punished so?" they cried inwardly;
>	"better that we had been banished to the Wilderness,
>	where at least the birds still sing,
>	than to endure this familiarity of Place
>	without any of the Essence that had made it Home,"
>	and they wept sorely, and could not be comforted,
>	even with one another.

But from across
the wooded Quadrangle
came finally a first sound again;
rather tentative, a basso sustenato
made its way through the leafless branches of the winter trees
and found its way through open windows
to pierce the Great Silence
holding the True Lovers against their will.
There followed the haunting choruses
of muted woodwinds and legato strings
and the Adagio grew ever louder as, one by one,
their instruments were tuned,
and cued into the Swell by the Prodigal conductor.
No, the Musicians hadn't abandoned their place on the stage,
but had remained hidden in shadow
throughout the Time of Exodus.
Knowing it would be the Poets who would return first
at the slightest recall of Beauty,

                                                    (more)

they had decided they could tolerate the Great Silence
no longer, and had picked up their instruments
in defiance, and unison,
and with heartfelt Compassion for the distressed True Lovers.

The True Lovers were finally consoled,
and as the grand Music played again and again,
they would scan the far horizons
each and every day,
watching for the return of their Imperial Court and subjects;
oh, some were already back,
reveling in the restored Order of Things.
But the True Lovers knew that others had lost their way,
and had vowed to one another to keep vigil
until the very Last Cello had been played out.
And somewhere inside themselves they knew
there would always be another Song,
another Song.

*John Gorman*
*North Miami, FL*

## AUNT LUCY

Evenings were Aunt Lucy's best time. She could sit in the rocker on her front porch and invite her memories to come calling. She could let go of Key West and 1900 and dance again with Robert in 1861. She could plan their wedding for the Saturday after she would finish at Madame Giraud's Academy.

"But the War came," she murmured, "and we had to rush everything. Graduation. So many weddings that spring."

She lingered over their few days together, intoxicated with each other and with the certainty of quick and easy Southern victory and an end to Yankee bullying. Then there were his leaves, each more frantic and more hurried than the last, and his uniform, first a lieutenant's, then a captain's and finally a major's, but always more threadbare and more in need of her mending. Then there was only the news from Chickamauga.

Her tears she cried alone. There were too many other women in black, half mad with shock and grief, and too much else to do in a land that was losing a war for its very existence. No one knew how she cut off the long blonde hair that Robert had loved so much, disguised herself as a teen-age corporal from a regiment destroyed at Vicksburg and rode scout across Georgia and the Carolinas for General Hood, the battered field glasses slung across her shoulder and a Colt revolver heavy on her hip. Twice, she shot her way through Union patrols, bullets whistling in her ears and the smell of black powder sharp in her nostrils. Those days, she tried not to remember.

When she came home after Appomattox, she found her family dead or scattered. Her hasty diploma from Madame Giraud's made her a school teacher, and she taught all eight grades in that one room for thirty years. She would have retired and died in Macon, if an uncle she hardly knew had not left her the tiny cottage she had decided to make her last home.

The afternoon story times were not really her idea, she told herself. But somehow the children had discovered that there was a genuine Southern Lady on Caroline Street who knew how things really were before the War between the States and baked cookies on Wednesday afternoons. It was they who called her "Aunt Lucy" and sometimes spoke to her of things their parents could not hear.

A photograph in the Key West Citizen on her lap caught her eye. The Knights of the Invisible Empire had held another convocation and burned another cross. The picture showed the hooded Klansmen standing stiffly beneath the stars and bars of the Confederacy, while the text below spoke of the "purity of Southern Womanhood" and "the black tide of evil."

"Poor white trash," Lucy muttered. She did not often allow herself such expletives, but the sight of "those ignoramuses in their silly costumes" seemed an insult to the flag Robert had died for.

Lucy was about to go inside, when Freddie Baker came around the corner at a dead run, slipped and fell, picked himself up without even a glance at his skinned knees and didn't stop until he had tumbled onto her porch.

"Aunt Lucy, Aunt Lucy," the eight-year-old wailed, "the White Hats!" he caught his breath. "The White Hats are hangin' Bobby Lucas down at the salt pond!"

"Bobby Lucas?" she wondered.

"He comes Wednesdays," Freddie panted. "He lives with his grandmother on Amelia Street."

The image of the unkempt twelve-year-old sprang to mind.

"Whatever for?" Lucy asked, rising slowly to her feet.

"They were gonna string up Rastas, the nigger who lives with that Spanish woman on Seminary Street, and Bobby heard 'em talking. When he had the fever, she prayed over him, and he got better. So Bobby went and warned them, and they got away in Rastas's boat. Now, the White Hats are so mad, they're stringin' up Bobby instead."

"Get the sheriff," Lucy ordered.

"He's gone up to Islasmorada after some wreckers, and nobody will listen to me. They're all afraid of..."

"Well, I'm not," Lucy snapped. "Fetch a horse, Freddie. I'll be right out."

A few steps brought her to the rolltop desk in her bedroom. The catch answered her fingers, the concealed drawer slid open, and the big cap-and-ball revolver was in her hand.

She turned up the kerosene lamp, sat down on the bed and began to load the pistol. Her hands were swift and skillful, but the stiffness in her fingers made putting the tiny primers on the cylinder slow work.

Only when she had finished did she allow herself to look at the tintype of the young man in the Confederate uniform that stood on the bureau. The tide of memories almost carried her away again, but she blinked back her tears, blew out the lamp and turned toward the door.

Freddie had found a horse. Lucy pulled herself into the saddle and helped Freddie get on in front of her. She thrust the revolver into the waistband of her skirt and covered the butt with her shawl.

"Guide the horse, Freddie," she commanded, giving him the reins. "I can't see too well in this light."

The aged mare was long past any hope of a gallop, but she did manage a fast trot. When Lucy saw the bonfire and the men gathered around it, she told Freddie to dismount and hide. Then she let the horse pick its way through the crowd.

The Klansmen were having too good a time to notice her at first. They had not bothered to tie Bobby's hands. They were just letting him dangle from the tree limb, clawing at the rope that was choking him. Some were passing a jug. Others were taking bets how long he would last.

Lucy squinted hard, but even her best glasses were not much help in the gloom. Then a hand reached up out of a white robe and took the bridle.

"What are you doin' here?" a thick voice demanded.

Even Lucy's weak eyes could see that far. She drew the revolver from under her shawl and cocked the hammer.

"You've had your fun," Lucy declared. "Now you let that boy down, or I'll kill you like a cur in the street."

There was a sudden silence as Lucy's finger tightened on the trigger. Any moment, a stone, a blow or a bullet might come out of the darkness, and all the will that remained in her was gathered in that finger. She felt the trigger soften as the rusty sear began to slip.

"Let him down!" the now-shrill voice beneath the hood cried.

Lucy caught the hammer with her thumb as it started to fall.

As soon as his feet touched the ground, Bobby threw off the noose and ran over to Lucy. She helped him onto the mare, and they rode slowly back to the street. There were a few muttered threats but no one made any move to stop them. Lucy took the boy to his grandmother and sat up the night with them, the old revolver in her lap.

By noon, the story was all over town, and it grew with every telling. The Invisible Empire was angry, and there were dark hints of revenge. But Lucy was the widow of a Confederate officer, and word was passed to leave her alone.

So indeed, she was left alone. But Key West was a very small place, and the Klan was very strong. Hardly anyone spoke to her, save in the course of business. The Wednesday afternoon cookies went uneaten, and even Bobby did not dare to come very often. When he turned fourteen and went to sea, even that company ceased. When Death came calling in the spring of 1906, Lucy had only her memories to keep vigil.

*Ryan McLaughlin*
*San Francisco, CA*

## TORNADOES

crazed people like to worship the tornado,
with its winds and hot breath so dragonlike, and
its brevity leaves them aghast —
floods and earthquakes and fires and drought and famine and
monsoons and volcanoes and blizzards and epidemic contagion
chaos.

"Isn't it exciting!" she said,
her gold tooth and her rags for clothes could not contain her
place in this catastrophe.
Any day that things don't change is a day that never was.
We can creep along and try to keep them for as long as they
will not rot in our hands or our teeth and our hair.

I was not surprised and I was not uncertain as to what she meant.
"Are you wishing more people would die?" I said,
my coat and tie dirty from the wind,
my coat and tie crumbling like I am inside of them.

Her mouth moved like an angry slug,
her hands shook as she shoved them in my pale face, burning
in the Midwest this orange-grey dustbowl sun.
"Can't you see this is HIS work and HE is COMING!"

This I bemoan as a sure sign of lunacy:
if GOD was a GOD he would not be such a dumbfuck to spare this
bitch.
"Your GOD licks and you'll be rotting in the ground someday
like the rest of us. There's no place for us to be rewarded
for spending our time shoveling someone else's shit," said I
as matter-of-factly as I could.

*Ryan McLaughlin*
*continued*

A mixed-breed dog limped by, shyly limping on a fractured leg.
I stooped down to pet the sad thing and decided I didn't want
to write this story.
I decided I didn't want to spend my life shoveling this literary
shit for no reward on this earth or beyond.
There's no reward in knowing.
There's no reward in thinking.
Freedom is hell and its curse is the cure for religion.
I took the dog home and fed it.

*

*J F Pytko*
*Laguna Hills, CA*

# J DOE

1.

Unknown to the hearths
and familiars of little gray houses
west of east, and southwind grandsires
who clowned with marauding damsels
in search of distress,
the Nameless One is laid to rest.

His easy hands are antler still;
the face is smooth as armor, reflecting
the stone turned toward palehorse
hills once colored by his early years
of following the Samaritan's code.
He envisioned lamps in night windows,

**(more)**

and listened for sunspot birds,
decorating the trash strewn meadows
with holidays of song.

        2.

In a city,
he found compassion packed in cans.
A laugh was valuable as a diamond.
Angst was the only political party.
His love scouts and hope messengers
were always ambushed by the devil
blessed, living dead.

In the third preface of a dawn,
he shared a dish with gutter dogs
and matchbook cats, and thought of
darkened windows and hills
covered with gauze.
He sensed a presence of rage,
rising from concealment, and heard
a cry of terror; and responding
to it took a knife intended
for another.
He fell into anonymous death
without a gesture or a word
to censor the image
of palehorse hills and the Spring
of his passage.

        3.

Around a city's trash can fires,
gut-hollow silhouettes dance
to the sounds of manhole covers.

**(more)**

Drummer-boy Death picks up the beat
as lights blow out.
By a road in a range of hills,
a window lamp spreads gold medallions
over fallen clouds of snow.

*

*Elizabeth Marchitti*
*Totowa, NJ*

## GREEN GRAPES

Eat green grapes in autumn, sweet, juicy,
remember how green began
with the maple buds in Spring,
pointed leaves of crocus and tulips
pushing through snow.
Savor the taste of early peas and tender green
onions, fresh from the garden in June.
Smell ocean salt, feel foam
swirling around ankles in July,
Dream the lush green of summer,
texture of tomato plants, odor
of leaves that lingers.
Recall neat rows of lettuce in
Grandpa's victory garden,
the smell of fresh-cut grass in August.

Listen, you might hear the rustle
of that dress of pale green taffeta
that Mother made for you when you were nine.
Turn quietly, you might see
that childhood Christmas tree, that glorious green,
when trees outside were bare,
and green was gone.

*Elizabeth Marchitti*
*Totowa, NJ*

## FOUND WEEKEND

Remember that weekend in October
when we went down to the shore?
It's a waste of time, you said,
it's too cold to swim.

But I was after quiet,
the smell of salt, sand in my shoes,
the waves to whisper to me,
        peace, peace, peace—

Why did we stand so long
on the landing of the motel
looking at Engleside Avenue?
Old buildings, faded, trimmed with gingerbread—
the rough touch of the railing,
weatherbeaten, wobbly—

No cars, no people,
    nothing
but a lone mockingbird,
mocking the seagulls.

*Don Thornton*
*New Iberia, LA*

## KAVORKIAN'S CURE

This fabric, thread worn,
ragged, a measure of time
reflected in eyes of lemmings
as they rush to the sea
crazed by smells of salt &
promises of life eternal
where rodents rule supreme
and nights ring with crickets.
This instinct for suicide
unravels, a thread of road
into dark, dense forest
from whence none return
and no records are kept.
Overwhelmed by instinct
to be and not ask why,
driven by intuitive fears,
synonyms unlisted, unknown
urges pressing to surface,
floating on waves of dreams,
icebergs mostly submerged
with glistening, white caps
bobbing above dark waters.
Death wish as catharsis.

*William Rose*
*Brooklyn, NY*

## THE DAY IT RAINED MONEY

It was a day like any other day in Northern Mexico when Juan Rivera crossed the Rio Bravo and found himself on the other side of the border. He'd lost his hat, the sun was hammering down on his bare head, his clothes were soaked and in tatters from the concertina wire he'd had to crawl under, but he'd made it. He was in the Promised Land.

So actually it was a very special day for Juan: the beginning of a new life with the possibility of giving his children enough food and sending money so the doctors would care for his mother. And, eventually, of being able to bring his wife and children north with him, legally, with a nice little house to live in. Juan expected new and unusual things to happen to him now, so he didn't think it was so strange when the dark clouds blew up from the west and the sky clouded over. That the desert should have rain wasn't strange on the day when all his wishes were beginning to come true.

Then it began to rain and Juan turned his face up to receive the cool benediction of heaven. But instead, he felt something rough passing over his skin. Rough and not at all cool or liquid. He opened his eyes, and then opened them some more. It wasn't water that was raining down but banknotes, and, sure enough, they were gringo banknotes. The smallest denomination was a fifty; then there were hundreds and thousands and even larger bills.

"Bendita sea la Virgen," Juan whispered to himself, crossing himself and kissing the crossed thumb and forefinger of his right hand. Obviously, the miracles had already begun.

So it was true what they said; in the United States it actually rained money in the streets.

Not that Juan was in a street, but that was a technicality that didn't bother him for a moment. Quickly he stuffed his pockets full of the biggest bills he could find, then his shirt until it bulged with dollars sticking out between the buttons.

As the money rained down it became harder and harder to walk uphill; it was like sloughing through a marsh. Finally, Juan reached the top of the ridge and saw a vast plain of scrub oak and pinon pine and sage bush spreading out before him in total desolation. At least there were no border guards or fierce guard dogs and everywhere there was money, huge piles of money. Juan stood there for a long time contemplating the sight in a state approaching mystic ecstasy, and then he realized something else, something a bit more sobering. Nowhere in that whole vast plain was there a place to spend all this money.

But there would be. And with a frenzied cry Juan ran forward toward the glittering cities that must lie just beyond this desolation; cities which welcomed men with money; cities with bright lights and beautiful women and plenty of tequila. Juan was now totally oblivious to the blazing desert sun which had broken through the clouds and again hammered on his bare head like a pile driver, or, indeed, to anything which stood between him and the satisfaction of his desires.

***

A dirty, tattered group of homeless crouched in their shacks under the East River Drive in New York City and waited for the rain to start. They left their shopping carts full of empty soda bottles and tin cans just outside the doors to their shanties (when they had doors) where they could keep an eye on them because the few cents they'd receive at the recycling center meant food for a night. The bottles weren't just bottles and the cans weren't just cans; they were life itself, survival in a cold, hostile world. So they watched them vigilantly, but there was no question of staying out in the rain. It was all very well when people hurrying home got wet because they could towel themselves off and take warm showers and change into dry clothes when they got to their apartments or town houses. But for this group all the clothes they had were on their backs, and it would take a long, cold time for them to dry.

"Just hope the damned thing don't collapse," said Pete, pointing to the cardboard roof of his shack with a finger twisted with arthritis.

"The highway'll protect us a little," said his neighbor Wilma Cohen. She was somewhere in the vicinity of seventy years old, and the only member of the little community they called Cohenville who remembered--or cared--what her last name was. That was why they'd named the settlement after her.

"Huh!" snorted Pete. "The cars slosh enough water over the edge to drown a duck."

"Well, we ain't ducks," said Wilma, and cackled with mirth. She wasn't really worried because she'd covered her roof with a sheet of corrugated steel she'd found somewhere in her wanderings through the nocturnal labyrinths of New York near the abandoned docks and warehouses.

Then she stopped laughing. What was falling was not water but bills, Hundreds, millions, billions of banknotes. It looked like Christmas time with money instead of snow falling from the sky.

"Holy shit," said Pete in an awed voice. "Damned if it ain't rainin' money. Look at all that beautiful bread, man."

"Let's get it," said Wilma, scrambling out of her shanty and stuffing the pockets of her coat and the various sweaters and numerous blouses she was wearing with bills.

"Where's it comin' from?" asked old James, who was doing the same thing a few houses over, except that he was so bent and twisted that he could hardly lean over and had to scrape the money together in piles with his ancient cane.

"Who cares?" said Wilma. "Maybe one of them armored cars rolled over and split open. What difference does it make? Just take it and run before somebody starts looking for it."

"Where?" asked Pete.

"To the supermarket, you fool," said Wilma. "That's where they got the food."

"Should we take our empties, too?" wondered Pete.

"Pete, sometimes I think you really are crazier than a hoot owl," said Wilma, stopping for a second and looking at her neighbor with her fists on her hips and a disgusted expression on her face. "What's the matter with you, boy? Don't you realize that we got more money here than we could get with a million of those lousy cans and bottles? We can have food now, and nice clothes and warm houses, just like everybody else. We're rich, Pete. Don't you know what that means? We're rich."

"Damned right," said James, "and I'm gittin' me down to that old Pathmark right now."

The whole group streamed after him: Wilma and Pete and just behind them Marygold nursing her skinny baby with a tit that had dried up months ago and Jose, who had a tattered Puerto Rican flag flying proudly over his shanty, and Randy, thin as a dry twig (he was in the last stages of AIDS, and no one could understand how he'd survived this long) and a few other residents of Cohenville. But when they reached the Pathmark they saw that it was besieged with angry people waving fistfuls of banknotes in the air.

"It ain't fair, Mancuso," a woman with long, dirty gray hair shouted. "Now that we got the money you won't sell us the food."

"Please, please," said Jerry Mancuso, the store manager, blocking the doorway with his short, tubby figure. "Don't you people understand? I ain't got no more food. It was sold out in the first ten minutes of this, this...whatever it is."

"That ain't true," shouted a man's voice. "You got it in the cellar changin' the prices. I bet you'll sell a jar of peanut butter for a thousand dollars now."

Jerry raised his arms and rolled his eyes to heaven. "What would I do that for?" he asked. "I got all the money I could ever hope for already. Me and the kids inside been collectin' it ever since it started fallin' and we're all millionaires. Why should I hold back on you?"

"He's lyin'," shouted another voice, so hoarse it was impossible to tell if it was a man's or a woman's. "Let's go in and take our food."

"Right!" roared the crowd, and with a mighty crash the glass windows caved in and people streamed through the gaping holes. Some stumbled and were ground into the shards of glass so that others tracked blood down the aisles, but no one noticed; all they noticed was that the shelves were empty.

"There's no food downstairs, neither," a group reported. "Where's Mancuso?" a man shouted. He was a burly biker with a black t-shirt cut off at the shoulders, an iron cross around his neck and a skull and crossbones tattooed on each burly forearm. "We'll cut his lousy throat if he don't tell us where the food is."

But Jerry was no longer on the scene. He had decided the moment of utter chaos was the best chance he'd have to disappear, and disappear he did.

Slowly the place emptied of people, their faces twisted with disappointment, but Wilma and Pete still walked slowly down the aisles, their shoes crunching in bloody glass, staring at the empty shelves with dazed expressions.

"Now if that don't beat all," Pete said, shaking his head from side to side.

"Yeah," said Wilma. She felt tired, and just wanted to sit down somewhere and cry.

"All this money and nuthin' to buy," said Pete, continuing his endless lament.

"Oh, shut up, Pete," said Wilma. "Just shut the fuck up."

***

Jan watched the terrace of their penthouse gradually fill with money. When she opened the door it tumbled inside the apartment like the piles of dry leaves she had leaped in when she was a kid.

"My God, Dick, come here," she cried.

"What is it?" yelled back her husband from the bedroom, where he was trying to knot his black tie in front of the mirror and having a frustrating time of it.

"You'd better come here," said Jan. "You're not going to believe it."

"And if you don't hurry up and get dressed we'll be late at the restaurant," said her husband. "This is a very important client, Jan. For God's sakes, show some consideration for my work."

"Your work," said Jan. She began to laugh until the tears ran down her face. Her high heels catching in the deep plush rug, she staggered backwards until she fell into the soft leather sofa, still laughing. "Your work," she repeated.

"Yes, my work," said Dick, walking into the living room, still fussing with his tie. "It just happens to be what pays the bills...oh, my God." His mouth fell open and he stood like a statue and gazed at the thick rain of banknotes falling into the deep canyons of the city. The living room floor was already ankle deep in banknotes that had spilled in from the terrace and Jan was now sitting in the middle of them, flinging handfuls into the air.

"Money," he said, kneeling down and crumpling some of the bills up in his hand. "It's real money. It's not a joke or a publicity gag, it's the real McCoy."

"You ought to know," gasped Jan, still choking with laughter. "You've done enough to get it."

"I don't understand," said Dick. "I just don't understand. What does it mean?"

**Dan River Anthology '95//27**

But Jan wasn't thinking about Dick or about money at that moment. She was thinking that in the little Ohio town where she grew up everyone raked leaves into huge piles in the fall to burn them. Those crisp evenings with the dusky air blue and fragrant with the smoke from the burning leaves were one of her favorite memories of childhood. Where had it all gone? she wondered.

Then Jan looked at Dick with repulsion on her face and said: "It means, for one thing, that I'm out of here. I've only put up with you for one reason, and now that reason is gone, baby, gone. And so am I. So long, Dick. Have fun with all your bucks. It's all you ever wanted, anyway."

Dick watched her walk out the door and slam it behind her back. His mouth was still open. Then he slowly looked back at the thick rain of banknotes. The living room was now knee-deep in money. Somehow Jan's leaving didn't seem important. Dick knelt and threw handfuls of it over him and laughed like a child. Then he scrambled to his feet, his face red with rage.

"It's not fair," he screamed. "Now that I've finally got it, so has every other prick. It's just not fair."

*Desoree Thompson*
*Beaumont, CA*

# PASSING OF AN ERA

I went to a going out of business sale today.
The demise of a dear old five and dime king.
Woolworths' stores are going to my dismay.
It was where I bought most everything.

I used to meet friends for lunch.
Triple Decker sandwich and soft drink.
Small price could feed a bunch.
Blue plate special served in a wink.

They had everything I could afford to buy.
Remember Blue Waltz perfume, hankies for mom.
Costume jewelry and for dad a necktie.
Cosmetics and hand cream, Italian Balm.

Woolworths' five and dime gone for good.
It's so sad it was my favorite store.
A place of dreams like Hollywood.
I'll never be able to go there anymore.

**Dan River Anthology '95//29**

*Anneke Mason*
*Tacoma, WA*

## NOAH'S TRIAL

No night was longer than this one on the endless
waves. Not even Cain, hiding from God's eye, saw
less light.

Surely this was an agony longer than the sting
of fire could have been, and darker than scorched
earth. Even parched clay, cracked and infertile
after constant drought would have been less dooming

For forty days and forty nights there was no difference between their
hours of waking and dreaming. The animals
in their cages would moan and stir uneasily, sensing
the artificiality of the light from oil wicks and having
trouble sleeping when Noah, deciding it must be night,
would extinguish even these small replicas
of the day's eye

Where Cain had not been able to outrun God's eye, Noah
looked for it constantly. But no light broke through
the shroud and no voice answered

After the Lord had shut him in, after the rains had
commenced, the voice of the Lord was heard no more
and his light left the earth

The rain thundered on the roof and beat against
small windows. The water rose steadily on the land,
and steadily the ark drifted farther and farther from
Noah's home. And all the earth was enveloped in vast
greyness, darker than nights of days gone by. All of
creation was a prison

As the noise of the beasts grew stronger, Shem, Ham
and Japheth grew more restless and their wives more
quarrelsome. And the silence in Noah's cabin grew louder

"Lord, how do we survive these lightless skies
and hourless times? Give us your sign, just one
slight sign...Do you intend to drive us mad?
Nothing is left of your creation, how then will
we survive?"
But the rains beat on and the day's eye was not
visible

"Lord, do not hide your face from me as Cain hid his
from you. I am offering to you all that we can spare
and more. May the fragrance of the oils and cakes
soften your heart..."
But the rains kept coming and there was no sign

"Lord, I wander the decks. The woman of my loins
is crying for companionship I can no longer give
her. Ham curses his wife and Japheth tries to
still her tears. Shem envies Cain's lot..."

"I am Yahweh" blew the wind and the rains subsided
and God's voice was in the warmth of the sun

*John Marrs*
*Boulder, CO*

## PATH OF THE HUNTER

A small wash meandering west rippled by wind, untracked.
Her voice, soft, rattling cottonwood leaves. Her countless
colors spilling into the distance.
    When does a man touch his past?
"It is as you perceive," a voice so distinct it jerked me
from my thoughts. There before me an ancient hunter crouched
with spear in hand. His hair loose and dark; his skin brown,
taught with muscle. His only covering a simple loin cloth. His
focus the near distance. He slowly turned, our eyes meeting,
our spirits becoming one; my skin a rush of sensations. As the
vision dissolved in its place lay an ancient cottonwood sun-
bleached and so very beautiful in its long sleep. I walked
to it and touched its weathered gray skin, spoke softly. The
voice spoke again, "It is as you perceive."

Before me lay a gray-white stone- raw stock for the making
of arrowheads and spear points. Its perfection and beauty so
exact there was no mistaking its significance.

I held it in my hands. I wondered how many tens of decades
it lay there. I held it up, its transparency filling with sunlight, such beauty
to be unlocked by the right hands. I placed it back on the sand, perhaps
another day and time my
past will teach my hands the secrets necessary.

    When does a man pass through the portal to become his past?
    When does he shed his false skin and become that which speaks
    loudest? When does he turn and embrace the truths of his life?

All the mysteries, the questions, the gifts, the answers, the

**(more)**

truths locked in stone. Before me a fleck of white in the
rippled sand, my hand reaching, my eyes remembering, my heart
knowing.

Path of the hunter—untracked, unknown, seasons of the moon
and sun—my footprints unhurried, quiet, naked of shoes gently
placed within his.

*

*Carol Ellms*
*Spencer, MA*

## THE MUSHROOM WILL COOK

Moira left it — that huge
black and gray ugliness —
soaking in pure spring water
poured into a paper cup
and covered with a napkin.
It has been there all day
on the kitchen counter.

Its bulging contours
shape thoughts of dark
and light, the yang
and yin of her faith
and hope that blend
the medical
and the macrobiotic.

She came with a Coleman stove
and a small propane tank,
bags of brown rice and beans,
jars of mushrooms and seeds,

(more)

kelp and herbs,
a wicker basket filled
with bone china plates
painted blue and gold,
and a pair of chopsticks.

Rising each day
before the moon sets,
she rides long highways
to reach radiation
treatments to shrink
soft tissue sarcoma
prior to surgery.

Tonight the mushroom will cook
outdoors on the Coleman stove
fueled by a small propane tank
attached to its side
and all the stars burning
in the distant night sky
will come near with their light.

*Patricia Greenwood*
*Schenectady, NY*

## ALMOST THERE

She escapes to the granary
to light a stale cigarette.

>Barely fourteen,
>puberty tingles up her spine.
>Some girls at school
>have had It.
>She imagines how It must be.

>>Smoke curls out the window
>>strains to touch birds she wishes
>>to be one.

She escapes from the granary
to inhale pear blossom aromas.

>Barely fourteen,
>puberty aches a well in her breast.
>Some girls at school
>are There.
>She imagines how There must feel.

>>Blossoms ripe with feminine scent
>>linger    in breezes  she wishes
>>>to be one
>>>to be whole
>>>to be There.

**Dan River Anthology '95//35**

*Sherry B. Hanson*
*Brunswick, ME*

# GIUSTIZIA!

All quiet the arena
a spit of white sand
lifts on a breeze,
caprice of the gods perhaps
before beasts and mortals swarm

A flourish of trumpets
standards to the wind
as one by one
each gate opens.
Behold the charioteers!

From Athens and Corinth,
Sidonia, Byzantium, the
tribune Messala from Rome
and the Jew Ben-Hur.
They've raised the field

Messala the scourge in
scarlet and gold with
his team of winged blacks

Hur in white and
star of David
and his white Arabians

All graceful chariots
light of wheel
burnished to please the gods

The governor drops his handkerchief

*Sherry B. Hanson*
*continued*

In less than a lap
the Athenian falls
victim of the Roman spike

The crowd roars madness but
Messala slashes on;
horse eyes pool in pain

Messala, evil in Roman gold
terrible force unleashed
to spike a chariot victory

Neck and neck the blacks and Arabians,
Messala's lash hisses and cuts
catches the Arabs of Hur!

The arena a fury
even the rats have left, the
gods thrown up their hands.
There is no law in
the circus at Antioch

But the white horse Antares
clasps the turn,
Rigel and Altair hold.
Aldebaran surges and
Hur takes the lead

Wicked Messala has
run his last race. Suddenly
tossed and trampled he lies
broken on the ground,
the blacks berserk in flight

*Sherry B. Hanson*
*continued*

with never a backward glance
and Hur comes round in victory.
Giustizia! Gloria!
The Gate of Triumph opens
and Rome crowns a Jew

*

*Marcie Leitzke*
*Lake Placid, FL*

# THE BROMELIADS

There they were
where the red bird sings:
a whole plot of bromeliads
almost hidden along the roadside
growing under palmettoes,
sage and brushpiles,
hidden, yet visible
once you saw them.

Then they were all you saw,
nothing but bromeliads,
then more and more,
like souls lost in tangles
almost buried amidst the clutter
of everyday things.

Kevin Lavey
Baltimore, MD

## A QUIET SATURDAY NIGHT

They'd begun sleeping together a month ago. Perhaps a week afterwards, while ascending the stairs to his third floor apartment, she said she had something to tell him.

"Something you should really know about," she said.

"Sounds ominous," he said.

"Ominous about hits it," she said.

Inside, he walked to the couch with two beers. He leaned back while she perched forward. Her straight brown hair hung below her shoulders and hid her face. She'd played tennis that afternoon and still wore her fuzzy yellow wrist band.

"I'm married," she said.

"Oh, come on."

"I'm married."

"Where's your husband been?"

"On a job up north."

"Christ," he said, and paused. "Do we stop?"

She turned to look at him. "No," she said.

Mark put the book down on the end table, walked to the kitchen, and poured himself another cup of coffee. He stayed home this Saturday night hoping Karen would call, but she hadn't.

He'd never had an 'affair' before. Something he couldn't imagine telling her was that only a year ago he was a virgin. The Catholic thing, an older brother of one of his friends once said to him, rips your balls off: you've got to find them and put them back on yourself. Mark was twenty-two.

He waited for the telephone to ring. Two rules: he wouldn't be possessive, they would continue until it couldn't be managed any longer. They met. She was married. No complications. Only very, very recently, maybe three days before, while lying alone in his room late at night, he began to question himself; he made himself say the awkward, obsolete words aloud: "Do not commit adultery." He had been raised a Catholic after all.

The phone remained silent; he picked it up to see if perhaps it was malfunctioning, but the dial tone buzzed. The quiet sounds of night swished up from the street: cars braked for the stop sign just below his apartment window, someone ran by in tennis shoes. In the moments when nothing else disturbed the night's calm, he could hear fading shouts coming from the basketball court blocks away. The odor of linseed oil he'd applied to a table that day lingered in the room.

He read a few more pages then rose from the couch and walked to the window which overlooked the residential street. Behind him the refrigerator's motor turned off and the quietness of the apartment rose like a tide change. He watched a Siamese cat sitting beneath the porchlight a few houses away lick its paws.

The phone rang. It creased the stillness of the room and he felt its vibration walk down the back of his throat. The last time she came over they drank wine together; then she had to leave and he could hardly sleep for thinking about her. It rang again.

"Hello," he said.

"Mark?" A woman's voice. His mother. "Mark?"

"Mom? Hi. Hi, how are you?"

"Mark?"

"Yes, Mom, it's me," he said.

"Mark honey, have you spoken with your sisters?" Her voice was breaking.

"No, no I haven't. What's going on there?"

"Your father's had a heart attack." She began to cry. "We don't know if he'll make it through tonight. Mark," she said, "it's a bad one. The priest gave him Extreme Unction."

She cried harder and harder until his own eyes became thick.

"Mom," he said, immediately thinking of flight schedules, immediately trying to comfort. "I'll try to get a plane to fly down there tonight, but that's probably not possible. We're so far away from the airport here. Are you listening to me? Otherwise, I'll take that one in the morning that I've taken before. Okay?"

"Yes," she said. "Yes."

"I'll come down. I've got to get hold of John Hansen at work to tell him I'll be gone for a few days. I have a feeling that I'm not going to be able to get a flight until the morning. It gets in around noon."

"Your brother will pick you up," she said.

"Listen, Mom, just let me get there by myself, all right? I'll get a cab in."

"Mark," she said, "pray for your father."

"I will," he lied. He'd not prayed in years. "Mom, listen, is Steven there now? Where are you?"

"We're at the hospital."

"Let me talk to Steven," he said.

His brother sounded numb. Mark found out that his sisters were trying to get flights in that night, but they themselves might not be able to arrive until the morning. He talked with his mother again and told her that he loved her and that he'd see her soon, then they hung up.

Damn it, he thought. Where is she?

He looked at the silent phone: a small, beige turtle crouched in its shell. He picked the receiver up and dialed.

"Hello," came a man's voice.

"Yes, is Thomas there?" Mark asked.

"No, he's not. He left a couple of hours ago."

"By chance do you know where he went?"

"No, I don't. I think he went out of town."

"Okay," he said.

He began to dial another friend's number but decided against it. He leaned into the chair and, as he knew he must, but wished not to, thought of his father. He looked at him as though standing at bedside: intravenous tubes dangling from an aluminum stand that resembled a hat tree threaded their way into his arm, his nose, one disappeared into the crotch of his hospital gown. Mark came to his face. His eyes were closed but his sleep was disturbed, the left cheek twitched, the right eye fluttered like a butterfly, the lips pinched shut. Mark called to him, but, of course, was met with silence.

He was already twenty-two, yet he and his father had only recently found themselves in a truce. They spoke together on the phone once in a while now and exchanged infrequent letters. What exactly they'd fought about for so long had become hidden beneath habit, and thus become abstract. Mark would only have to recreate to himself the sound of his father's voice or the sight of cigar smoke rising from behind the shielding newspaper or show himself any number of the thousand mental plates stored in his memory to feel in his stomach the tight wrench of anger, of sometimes even hate. He'd wanted their war to stop, he'd decided, it could not go on, but he knew that the man still towered over him. Mark couldn't keep himself from thinking it. What if he were gone?

He moved away from the window and sat down. His father lay on the hospital table, suspiring sounds seemed to emanate from the air itself, his chest rose and fell, gently, slowly. He was naked beneath the hospital gown. His feet were bare and faintly bluish, his hands were folded together, his face had become slack and peaceful and only briefly was he stretched out in immobility. Soon he was dead.

Mark rubbed his eyes with the tips of his fingers, washing the image away.

But he saw the chest flatten, expire, and in that moment, Mark was released. He floated, ascended as one does in dreams. Below him receded the museum within which was stored the clean, well-lighted exhibit, Father and Son.

Again he looked at the phone. It was now central to the room, it had become the vortex around which all the big space revolved. He walked to the window again and stood in the exact spot, in precisely the same position he'd been in when the phone rang earlier. The cat had disappeared.

He thought of Karen's husband, Howard, who probably held her close to him this minute while she slept buried in his chest. Howard might be awake, suspecting crimes of his wife he could hardly bring himself to consider. Perhaps Karen needed to break from her affair with him. Perhaps she was out walking in her neighborhood, listening to the night wind in the trees, smelling the flowers, confessing to herself what she promised she'd never do again. But maybe she simply let the night slip frivolously through her fingers not thinking or deciding or wondering anything, let it sift away like sand in an idle gesture on the beach. He needed badly to tell her of his father sprawled in a hospital about to die. She could not yet know how the sixth commandment and his father and he and she belonged to one another: that the sixth lived by the breath of his father whispered to him beneath archways and fantastic stained glass windows. The phone remained silent. In his mind played the ritualized struggle between son and father while from the darkness of the theatre's edge was a perfect oval, the mask of a woman's face softly, almost tenderly, lighted, watching, filling him with hope.

*Lu Spurlock*
*Bedford, TX*

## COMPANY MAN

The correct smile
played across his face
when he looked
at the president
and said
"Yes sir
I agree wholeheartedly."

It lingered
when

he bought his wife a mink coat
wriggled his toes
in alligator shoes

dieted
because the president
didn't like paunches.

Still smiling
at his retirement dinner
he fingered nitro
in his Brooks Brothers pocket.

*Sylvia Relation*
*Barre, VT*

# SPRING

Sun pokes through pleats in the blind,
casting light on the nicked aluminum bat
standing among its wooden cousins.
His dusty glove hovers over baseballs
spilling from a duffel.

I remember those endless nights
of indoor practice,
waiting for him, the motor running,
as Spring's muddy scent trickled by day
and froze over with darkness.

He survived tryouts and team cuts,
his dry palms cracked and bleeding,
we balmed them every night,
hoping they would heal before
the next throw thudded into his glove.

Daylight saving time and he practiced outside,
cleats squishing in the field,
night meeting the border of day,
we watched him trudge to the car,
muddy gum bag soggy on his shoulder.

The season arrived,
and we lived with pick-up suppers,
rainouts, no-hitters, the constant
drone of the washing machine
until
mid-July blazed the empty field,
the stained uniform hung in the closet,
cleats rested in a corner, stiff and dry,
hands healed,
waiting
for another Spring.

Ralph Pezzullo
New York, NY

## POEM ABOUT JESSIE

There was a river opening in your eyes
Clear and uncomplicated
So I followed it to its source
Leapt in and descended
Into the spiral magic
Where I was greeted by so many demons
Who nodded like friends
And after all the introductions
Led me to a flat green field
Where we watched a strange opaque sky
Turn purple
As a beautiful voice sang plaintively
Begging for deliverance
From furtive vines of guilt
And long self-pity
For the will to heal
Pits of ignorance and false belief
Tears of saints started falling on our faces
With mothers crying all around us
Boys kicking a ball back and forth in anger
Fathers screaming from the sidelines
Pulling out their hair
Drowning out the voice
But I listened
And I listened hard
Because it was unmistakably
You

*Emily W. Robinson*
*Kensington, MD*

## GETAWAY

My chalet is quiet
high
on the mountain
miles
from phones.
The smell
of burning pine,
and fragrant tea
welcome
my weariness.
Outside, sunshine
casts forest shadows
on fresh snow.
A calmness
settles into my afternoon.

Joyce S. Mettelman
New Hartford, NY

## BAT MITZVAH

Up wide stone steps bisected by an iron railing to the large, curtained doors. Then another five steps to the lobby, where two men in yarmulkas and prayer shawls guard the synagogue doors.
Dark red tile underfoot. Carved wooden box holding assorted yarmulkas. I enter: an usher hands me two books, one blue, one black. The synagogue is a vast stone, dome-ceilinged place with tall stained glass windows lining the left wall. Short stained glass windows above a series of metal plaques make up the right wall. In between, rows and rows of wooden pews; gold carpet underfoot. At the front of the temple, a pulpit where the Rabbi stands. Behind him, an alcove with paneled doors. The panels are decorated with symbols—wheat, flowers, branches. At either side of these panels is a heavily-carved chair. (I notice later that the Rabbi occupies one, the Cantor the other.) Several men, all wearing fringed white shawls, stand behind the pulpit. They take turns reading aloud in Hebrew in a singsong chant. They read from a huge, unrolled scroll lying across the pulpit. From time to time, the congregation murmurs "Amen" or rises in response to the Rabbi's gestures. Or reads aloud in English from a specified page.
Meanwhile, in the pews, little knots of people talk across each other or whisper together. An elderly shriveled man, his black yarmulka accentuating his white hair and chalk complexion, limps slowly down the center aisle; stops to embrace a friend or relative, then turns back to his seat. Two little girls about eight, in plaid skirts and sweaters, bounce down the aisle and exit. A tall bearded young man arrives and embraces everyone in the row ahead of me, which squeezes apart to give him space. Within minutes, I know that his name is Dave, he is home from college and the Bat Mitzvah girl is his cousin. Also, he is an anthropology major. To my right across an aisle, a sharp-faced young woman with graying hair and a shabby collar turns, glares fiercely at the talkative Dave and holds her index finger to her lips. Dave does not see her, but I do. (I am tempted to use my index finger in a different sort of symbolic gesture).
We rise again; there is a sort of rhythm to it. Sit down, murmur

Hebrew phrases (which are translated in my book into an English nearly as unintelligible) for several minutes along with the reader up there on the pulpit, then rise as the Rabbi opens the panels. Inside are two large scrolls; he turns to face them. We listen as he intones another prayer, then sit down again when he closes the panels. It goes on and on. He tells us to turn to page 131. I turn. He says to read aloud with him. I read. What does it mean? He announces that he will now turn over the service to Laurie; that her portion to read is about Joshua, and if we will turn to page 243 in the other book, we will understand why it is fitting that she is reading this on the day of her Bat Mitzvah. I turn to page 243, read the preface, and do not understand a single sentence.

A small figure in navy blue walks slowly up the two steps to the pulpit, climbs up on what must be a box and lo—the congregation can see the tiny face above the pulpit. I recognize her: it is Laurie, my friend's daughter; she looks pale and nervous. I cannot see the freckles, but I know they must stand out fiercely in that white face. In a clear, high voice Laurie begins to sing some Hebrew words. Yes, that is Laurie. But what is she saying? Does she know? She seems to, for she sings and sings, reading from the huge scroll in front of her with apparent ease. People all around me are suddenly quiet, intent, studying the Hebrew that she is reading, some singing softly along under their breath. She pauses, takes another breath, begins again. The large, white haired bulk of a woman sitting directly in front of me turns to her neighbor, smiles and nods her head in approval.

Suddenly, Laurie is finished. The Rabbi comes forward and delivers congratulations to her, her parents, her brother and sister, plus a brief sermonette on making life beautiful around her. He mentions that her mother is an artist and ties that in too. Throughout all this, he looks her in the eyes, but she looks right back, unwavering. She accepts a Bible from him, some candlesticks from a smartly-dressed President of the Sisterhood, then returns to her seat in the front row. I look around, expecting it to be all over, but the congregation continues reading, murmuring and talking for another half hour. Finally, we all rise, everyone sings a hymn they all seem to know. This is the only time they seem sure enough of the words to sing loud, coming in especially strong on the chorus. People turn to their neighbors, murmur a phrase which I find out later is "Good Shabos", meaning "Have a Happy Sabbath," and begin gathering gloves, coats and handbags.

I begin to understand the meaning of the word "exodus". As I edge out of my pew, I am caught in a tide of people spilling out of the synagogue. They all seem to know each other, and everyone begins to talk at once. Out in the lobby I cannot move. I stand there, pushed forward by the crowd. (Luckily, I notice before I am about to descend some stairs). This must be where I am supposed to go for the "Kiddush". Barbara, my friend, has explained this to me: they serve wine and cookies downstairs. The horde of people deposits me, like a shell cast up by the tide, at a doorway. I greet Barbara, her husband Paul, Laurie, her brother and sister and assorted grandparents, shaking hands but not quite knowing what to say. Those ahead of me have said, "Wasn't she wonderful?" already and, anyhow, how should I know if she was wonderful? So I just smile and continue along the line. I hug Laurie who is visibly relieved; her freckles have receded.

I watch as she holds a cup of wine aloft, says a Hebrew prayer along with the Rabbi and Cantor. I drink my tiny paper cupful of wine down in one gulp — too sweet. The long table, spread with a white cloth and platter after platter of petit fours, cookies, tiny cup cakes and slices of cake, beckons me. I take one petit four, almost too pretty to eat, before I am shoved backwards by a throng of new, eager eaters. Within minutes, the table is picked bare by hundreds of busy hands.

Munching the sugary cake, I weave my way back through the crowd. Everyone who *is* not eating is talking. Everyone who is eating is talking. Little groups of people are arranged everywhere in the long, narrow room, kissing, hugging, talking, introducing, drinking, telling stories, interrupting and, occasionally, listening.

It's catching. I move toward a group, introduce myself as Barbara's friend and open with, "Wasn't she wonderful?"

*Kay Renz*
*Santa Rosa, CA*

## ROOT WOMAN

"Blast ye!" Creatures of doubt! I'll not have ye downcast looks!
It be the dawning of a new age, and I be in trouble,
my lover, shanghaied by blokes bound
I know not where

Named for the Virgin, and not willing to bring
the town's eyes and tongues to your Christian family,
Agnes Mary, you packed your tapestry bags, crystal
and grandmother's shawl.
To protect your balance along the rocky road
you took your grandfather's old oak shillelagh.

A girl barely sixteen you crossed the sea to the New World
from the land where Wicca children once ran free in woods & meadows,
Where wee folk danced and rainbows were protected.

As indentured maid, for a trader family
you drove a mule to Indian villages, carrying cloth
and metal pots to the women.
The chief named you, "One Whose Hair Burst Into Flame."
With these people you made a life,
birthing your baby into medicine woman's cupped palms.

When the man your daughter knew all her life as father died, Agnes Mary,
you tore the fire from your scalp
ran deep into the forest where plants and animals helped you to heal.
Pale ones called you "mad," said you'd lost your mind
but to the people, you'd found wisdom.

At campfire gatherings, you shook that gnarly old stick

**(more)**

adorned with animal bones and feathers over head.
Flames crackling your chants, you danced to the six direction,
You'd say, "Wee ones, ye carry seeds of all the powers.
Fey! Use ye wisdom well!"

Now, on nights when the full moon lures me into her beam,
I see your talons pointing to me and my sisters, Agnes Mary.
Fire Hair, you crossed the ocean to a heathen land and found a home.
Grandmother, your roots spirit your daughter's daughters to sing their dreams.

\*

*Olivia Diamond*
*Rockford, IL*

# MINDSCAPE

Inner city where old thoughts become moths;
The pain that's claimed you is a tapeworm
winding down three flights of stairs there.
You'll never be the same again in
this cleanswept room within a dustball.
This is the hall of three arches, the pure air
within the speck of dust on the end table
in the grooves of your brass lampstand.
These motes are more alive than you are
in the sunlit hours of an April afternoon.
There the spores incubate in teensy dirt mounds.
Life germinates in the beginning of earth.
Potatoes sprout and seeds emerge from tips
of carefully compacted conical cribs.
There is where all my dead ideas are reborn
into something spanking new and will ascend
in linear runways out the archway of my room

(more)

into a landscape having no earthly horizon
or lines, because I choose the limitless
and lit spears of grass to grow from nowhere
in the collected detritus upon a concrete floor.
This room is roofless and wallless to allow
free thought to aerate the chambers of desire,
the primeval seed from which all life arises.
You've swept the chamber clean, sprayed well
all steps leading to a non-existent second floor.
You've sanitized and scrubbed the pillars,
kept the motif of grief company for hours
in a sad breviary of necessity, all alone.
In the dustball you are born to the dust
you return to rake up a second life.
Never alone even in a spotless room,
never alone in the silence of your heart.
The moth keeps its watch and climbs a wall
reaching for the light larger than life
in a landscape within a horizon.

\*

## RUDI HERNANDEZ

Rudi, the guide, climbs the temple in easy stride
where Toltec chieftain's jewels caught the sun,
where now I pant to the pyramid's peak allied
with time and space fusing into organic one.

He sits in noontide, his smile broad and brown
as I reach where he waits, burnished in the sun,
while I, beaming, one step at a time, come down
to where his eighty-five summers melt into one.

*Olivia Diamond*
*continued*

He says I look young as red-faced I reach him:
"You're thirteen; virgin of the Sun; in another
life you drew forth fire from sinewy limb."
then in his face, I discover a young lover.

The blue Aztecan sky washes over us
brightening the lens of my camera's eye.
When I focus, the plumed serpent flashes
in the ascent I wish to immortalize.

Criss-crossing the valley where the dead walk,
it's not the sun that shines in Rudi's eyes
or that makes me hear hewn stones begin to talk,
but the force of the pyramid which arises

in me like the snake growing the wings it must.
Rudi asks me what's the secret of long life
as he bends to pick a yellow rock from the dust
I mumble it must be good food, lack of strife.

At such response he shakes his head impatiently.
"No, it's the pyramid — Cleopatra's potion,"
then circumnavigates the rock rhythmically
over his body in a geography of the ocean.

*Renee Goldberg*
*Lido Beach, NY*

## THE BEACH PEOPLE

We enter the half-opened gate
ignoring the no trespassing sign.
A giant shroud enfolds us—blanket of despair.
The mourners of summer
face the inevitable.

Forebodings abound:
a child's sand pail—without a handle—without a child.
Here and there we see
lopsided abandoned umbrellas that have lost
the strength to stand erect;
beach chairs unraveled, unstrung,
once thrones on a summer's day.

A gray cloud of seagulls hang in the sky
like the albatross that hovers.
Some come down and flap at overloaded garbage pails
picking at pieces, shredding, aiming their beaks
through the meshed metal.
The gulls have grown fat from our crumbs.
They always wore a haughty look—beady eyes
looking askance.
They will miss us.

The ocean mocks
looking like a ruffled silver bed but
turning cold, then colder.
The timetable of the tides has altered.
The sun taunts—hiding behind haze or blazing
intently—breathing in and out, and out again

**(more)**

breaking its promise of earlier summer days
its power waning.

We inhale the last drops of sun
praying they touch us
(as if this star will never shine again).
By May we shed the shroud
and step into sunlight.

*

*Thomas Plante*
*Burnsville, MN*

# HAND MADE IN BRAZIL

I stare at the elephant with the curved tusks
as he moves ponderously
his back swaddled in a silver saddle
sparkling like a sequined gown
worn by Liza Minneli at the Academy Awards
but then it might remind you of the pomp displayed
at the most recent Pakistani election
of Banazir Bhutto
or the halycon years of the British Raj
as described by Rudyard Kipling
and you can almost see this elfin man
in starched white tunic and
elegantly turbaned head
the reincarnation of Gunga Din
riding astride this beast of burden
created by the artist Jobi
his torso covered regally by fine green pieces
of chipped glass

*Ginger Roberts*
*Setauket, NY*

## WINTERTIME BLUES
*for Richard*

Your silken form
casts a long shadow
across the ice

Ice again,
Ice floating and fetching up
in our harbor.
Ice in floes,
in riffs
in chilly winter blues.

Standing high
on the headlands,
I can see you are painting,
etching the shapes
of snowflakes,
and silhouettes
of eels frozen
in West Meadow creek.

Your fingers
measure the distance
between waves and sky.
The blue spaces
you outline
in violet shades
of night.

And flashing up
from your palette,
that tender, frightening
light.

*Alan C. March*
*Cincinnati, OH*

## GRANDPA'S VIOLIN

"If you don't take the violin, I'll just throw it away."
"Don't do that, Gramma," said Tom. "I'll take it."
I cut in, "Heck, give it to Goodwill. Get a receipt and take the tax deduction."
I chewed on my roast beef and tried to figure the value of an old violin. Probably not much, unless it's a Stradivarius. Grandpa's wasn't.
"I didn't know Grandpa was a musician," I said.
"He was a self taught musician," said Dad. "No formal training, played by ear. He played a couple of instruments." Dad took a swallow of milk. "Mom, do you still have his accordions?"
"They were Hohners, weren't they? Let me see..." Gramma rummaged through her mind's attic trying to locate the accordians. The memory attic of an eighty-four-year-old grandmother is a crowded place. Sorting through a lifetime collection of odds and ends can make finding a specific thing quite a chore. "Oh. I think I gave them away. Didn't Danny get them?"
As I ate my lunch, I thought of Grandpa, sitting in his chair ignoring the sounds and smells of the nursing home he now lives in. His head, almost completely bald, hangs so his chin nearly rests on his chest. He wears pajamas all day, but he is always cleanly shaved. And his mustache. His dashing pencil thin mustache, as ever, neatly groomed. I sighed and wished he were eating lunch with us like he used to.
"Did he play much?" I asked.
Gramma looked at me as if I were speaking Swahili.
"The violin, I mean. Did Grandpa play it very much?"
"Oh." She nodded slightly and her eyes opened just a little wider. They brightened, catching a sunbeam that came in the dining room window. "He played when we were very young. A long time ago."
I tried to picture Grandpa playing the violin. The Parkinson's has taken its toll. The slight tremors of a few years ago have grown. His medicine controls it sometimes, but the medicine makes him sick and weak. His hands tremble from disease or hang limply from medication.

**Dan River Anthology '95//57**

The image of his hand holding a violin bow eluded me.

"When we were courting, Grandpa would call me on the telephone," A smile indicated Gramma had uncovered another memory in her attic. "He would serenade me over the telephone by playing his violin."

I grinned at the confidence that must have taken. A young man in the 1920's, trying to impress his girl. With a violin resolutely tucked under his chin, bow in hand, he played to an old desk top telephone that stared back at him like a black daffodil. What a sense of romance he had. I ate a potato.

"Our telephone line was a party line. When Grandpa played his music, a neighbor who shared the line would pick her telephone up and yell at him saying, 'Stop that racket' so she could use the phone." Gramma smiled, "But he played the music for me; he always kept playing till he was through."

Gramma held her fork just above her lunch plate and stared across the table.

"Was he any good on the violin?" I asked.

"Oh heavens, no." The stare dissolved into another smile. "But I enjoyed it so." Mom passed the Jell-O fruit mold while Gramma continued talking.

"Grandpa and I met at a dance. The German-American Society held dances every other Saturday night. It helped many of us feel more at home sharing music and hearing the language."

I shook my head; Gramma and Grandpa at a dance in the 1920's? But they weren't grey haired grandparents then. They were kids who liked music and socializing and dancing. I wondered what music was played at the dances. German Polkas? Maybe they danced to the sounds of Bix Beiderbecke or Nick La Rocca's Dixieland Jazz Band.

Gramma as a flapper? I looked at her. Her hair was that grey-blue-white I've seen on her head for decades, but it was perfectly styled. She's always dressed sharp. I looked past some wrinkles and a few decades; yeah, I could see it.

Could Grandpa have been Gramma's escort to those Saturday night dances long ago? Now he sits in an electric lift-chair watching the Price is Right. His body is motionless with age and fatigue, but his shoulders are still broad.

I pictured those broad shoulders, strong and square, filling out a double breasted suit coat. The suit was chocolate brown and pin striped.

His pants must have been pleated, with a one inch cuff at the bottom.

I could see him confidently walking into the dance hall, his shiny brown shoes clicking across the hardwood floor. Young women standing along the wall smiled as he walked by. He smiled back and with a finger gently smoothed his Douglas Fairbanks mustache.

I could see him asking her to dance. She quietly accepted and he took her hand. He led her through the crowd, hand in hand, to the dance floor. Maybe they danced the Charleston. Or perhaps they danced together slowly to the sweet melodic song of a solo violin.

"Well," said Gramma. She let out a long, slow breath. "We don't dance any more." She was finished rummaging through her memory attic.

Ah, but one time they danced. I could picture it now.

"Gramma," I said, "let's keep the violin."

*Sol Rubin*
*New York, NY*

## THE SEAGULL

The restless tide plays
through wind-swept feathers,
hungry waves invade
the stricken bird
his eclipsed eyes
stare at passing clouds
memorized paths of heaven,
span carefree heights
feel the heartbeat-rhythm
of endless spaciousness.
Now the hazy sun paints
an orange horizon
above helpless wings.

A frenzied ocean sweeps
a baby shell
that lost its way
reaching my children,
make-believe architects
of soft castles
who pause and gaze
at a seagull
with motionless wings.

## LONG BEACH SOUNDINGS

Distant yelps of car alarms
snap at the night's mumblings.
Shoreline Village
vacant
locked shops
conspiring with salt-laden sea breezes
to swallow cryptic sounds.
Swells lazily drool
between Catalina rocks worn smooth
with watery words no ears can decode.

Our unformed questions never crash dramatically,
just ooze liquid meanings between knuckles
of the most tightly clenched fist.

No roared responses,
more a muted gulp
like a choked-down sob
that lodges mid-throat
or the syllables that slide back onto our tongues
if we shoot them upwind,
against the tide.

*Marijane G. Ricketts*
*Kensington, MD*

# YOUR NARROW ESCAPE

If only I could have taped
that clipflash on 26 —
your face, I'm sure of it!

Forehead and cheeks a puzzlement
of 60's peacemarks,
you're smiling mile-wide
whizz-close to a train
rushing boys off to Vietnam, I bet.

How could you, ecstasy itself:
Your only brother already there
on the Midway. He, invisible
as pain, till the day his face
ghosts our phone again.

You and that mumblemouth chef
out of Michelle's,
putting wordsworth together —
a pine-paneled cabin dug in
under Mount Saint Helens, about
as far as you'd make it away
from East Coasters, I'd say.

But you must have over-ranted it
(I always knew you would),
must have exploded, split up,
before Helens' rampage, thank God!

I'm squint-eye positive that's your face.
Why can't I ever remember,
can't make myself ask?

*Mary Engel*
*North Bergen, NJ*

## KING DAVID'S TOMB

You lie in splendor, a paler pharaoh, eyes
no longer seeking an errant Saul. The past,
sealed with Kings commanding the sun to rise,
still haunts the hall where Jesus ate His last
supper (Golgotha the final sting).
You broke the covenant when you ruled with fire.
Your hands hang at your side; they cannot bring
the cup to your lips, wield a sword, play the lyre.
You slew the giant with the strength of your arms.
But now whose song do you sing: The shibboleth
of kings is buried with Bathsheba's charms.
Old man, betrayed, you copulate with death.
Frayed memories of Absalom's cold schemes
will never thread the tapestry of dreams.

\* The Hall of the Last Supper is located in the upper story
of David's building which contains David's cenotaph.

**Dan River Anthology '95//63**

*Irene G. Dayton*
*East Flat Rock, NC*

## ANXIETIES DIE HARD

Anxieties die hard
for they embrace
sheltered coves
catching
pale and fragmented
light-rays in tenuous
and hidden holes.
Like turbulent
streams pouring
from a flood,
imploding upheavals
wash over weathered
rocks and worn
footholds. Soon they
burrow into deep and
submerged caverns
until new traumas
and old release
an uncomforting
grip to channel
through fire-falls
of prismed light.

Ancient symbols and
inherent speech
etch down
through innumerable
unspoken memories
where unconscious
desires surge in a

**(more)**

crystal rendering
of dream.
Old tales embody
new themes. And like
April hills spawning
with budding
leaves, symbols and
anxieties abound
into a life
invigorating assurance.

*

*David Norris*
*Seoul, Korea*

## HYUN JOO'S LOVER

She brings flowers on Sundays
Places them in your vase
Her body an amber lamp
Red gold against your pillow

She laughs at your nonsense
Listens intently to your stories
Cooks foods you cannot name
Strawberries in cream for dessert

And then loves you again
Laughing before she kisses you
Knowing you will not meet
Like this until next week

Makes the bed, smoothes out
The wrinkles, leaves the roses

*Phyllis de la Garza*
*Willcox, AZ*

## THE AUCTION

I did not know you, Mrs. Josey,
living around the corner from me.
I admired your pink house surrounded
by cholla and prickly pear when I jogged
around the block on hot summer nights.

Noticing the flickering blue TV light, I
wondered who lived there. I never saw you
in the yard. I did not bother to inquire.

Yesterday on my way to the post office
I saw cars and trucks in your yard.
Men carried furniture out of the house.
I thought it was a yard sale. But no.
The auctioneer said you died last week.
He joked about your being ninety-five
and never parting with anything.
Your heirs were selling out. A yard sale?
No. Tomorrow is the auction.

I snooped briefly through boxes, wooden barrels,
storage cabinets and chests. Artificial flowers,
dog collars, antiquated electric fans with greasy
frayed cords. Picture puzzles, glassware and shoes.
Costume jewelry, mirrors and electric teapots.
Each tagged with numbers. Impersonal.

I went home. In the morning the auctioneer's yodel
blared throughout the neighborhood.
I dropped my garden tools. I joined the crowd.

**(more)**

Fi-dolla-fi-dolla-fi-dolla? Sold!
Five dollars.

A strong wind came up. Nobody cared.
Lot by lot, the auctioneer joked, explained,
entertained. A showman, smooth, just
trying to make a buck. A blue-grey wig.
Two-dolla-two-dolla-two-dolla? Sold!
Two dollars.

I thought of you, Mrs. Josey,
a lady I'd never met. Children jumped
on your hide-a-bed. Curious adults
poked through photo albums.
We were good neighbors.
We never bothered each other.

I hung around until the very end. Seven hours.
Leaning against a dumpster in the wind.
I had not meant to do that. I even went
without lunch. But they made jokes
about your bed pan. It sold for fifty-cents.
I did not see the humor at all.

Last to sell was your clothing. 1920s party dresses
hung defenselessly in the wind all day. Stroked and
squeezed. An interested buyer said she planned to
cut them up for doll clothing if she could get them
cheaply enough. I rescued your mother's 1890s
black silk cape. And your father's black cutaway
coat. You saved them all these years. I bid on them.
I got them.

I did not know you in life, Mrs. Josey. But your
mother's cape and your father's top coat will
hang safely in my closet.
Until my heirs hold an auction.

**Dan River Anthology '95//67**

*Gwendolyn Carr*
*Magnolia, MA*

# HOMEWORK

The dawning day hurries her along—
the child to feed,
the beds to fold,
the dishes in the loud machine
remind her of the empty cup
she shoved beneath the bed.
Returning to the kitchen,
supper simmers on her mind,
the grocery note grows longer,
begonias droop, look thirsty.
Oops! a nasty river on the sill
reflecting in the window glass
the dust of this dry summer.
Then, choosing from
a waiting list
one of many urgencies,
she counts the reasons why
her day will not contain it,
and turns her tired body
to the chair that never fails
to rock her in its yellow arms
as if it understood

John W. Gracy
Brooksville, FL

## THE CALL

I've just turned sixty. The months seem to have fewer days, and the days fewer hours than they had when I was fifteen back in nineteen forty-seven. Then, each day stretched out like the perspective in a Dali painting, and, at the Catholic school I attended, that was the definition of life, a road running to the horizon where it met the infinity of a cool, disciplined, azure blue heaven. Today, I kiss my wife and point the car down a grey concrete, interstate highway to the place where I work.

I have traveled that road for ten years, so that I need pay attention to the traffic only at the two places where other roads cross mine. The distance between cars is automatic. The only variations are the wrecks along the road, about three a year. Since the car radio is broken, my mind wanders through the years of my life and concentrates again and again on the turns that have brought me to this particular road.

Each of those memories pulls and is pulled by others. They are more like a train than like an avalanche. This train is a toy whose locomotive and caboose are unseen behind a mental bend and whose off switch is broken so that it never stops.

My journey began its shape forty-five years ago. The ordinary details of that day have been lost in that growing haze that mixes years and events, and rubs the edges off times and faces. It was spring. The sun was shining, but whether it was April or May is lost.

The heart of the remembered moment has me on my knees watching the red light of a candle glowing and swaying slowly back and forth in the dark above the sanctuary of our parish church. The light from the 19th Century Bavarian stained glass windows pushed through the gloom for only a few feet along the side aisles so that the windows shone like frames taken from a technicolor film in a darkened movie theatre. The afternoon sun had not yet struck the windows along the back of the sanctuary wall above the wooden altar painted white with grey striations to look like marble. The Christ hanging from the cross in those windows had a body as pale as the white cloth draped around his waist. He was bloodless and dead. The window on his right held Mary, weeping,

**Dan River Anthology '95//69**

clasping her hands and looking at the ground. To the left of the cross was the window with St. John in red and green staring up at the face of the dead Son of Man.

A red sanctuary light swayed above the altar. It was no ordinary lighted candle. As did all Catholic trained grade school children, I knew that this was the guarding angel before the face of God. I had seen and heard the eighty year old pastor of that parish, a man educated in the deep mysteries of theology, a leader, a man revered by my parents, a man who could forgive sins and change bread and wine into the body and blood of Jesus Christ, scold the little sister in charge of the sacristy until she wanted to hid her face as the rest of her was hidden in clouds of black serge and rosary beads because the candle in that red lamp had been allowed to go out during the night. The sisters in the grade school classes had explained that a burning candle must supply that light twenty-four hours a day, that an electric light bulb would not do, no matter how much more efficient it might be and no matter how many scoldings it might save the sister sacristan.

The light served notice that resting in that twelve inch by twelve inch space was the God who had created the universe in a mere six days. That candle was put out only two days of the year, Holy Thursday and Good Friday because, on those two days, the precious bread which was the body and blood, soul and divinity of Jesus, the dying Lord, was removed from its altar closet where it had been nested in gold laces and embroidery produced by the hands of the virgin nuns during the hours of their recreation.

As I knelt, I meditated, pondered, and prayed over what my fate in all the life ahead of me should be. Being fifteen and Catholic had a heavy and serious aspect in the years right after the crushingly just God had helped us, His chosen nation, destroy the Nazis and Japanese and while we were in dread of the Communist plot to infiltrate and take over the local county government. During World War II, at each year's novena, we were told that the rosary and the miraculous medal had already saved the lives of many soldiers and would save us from any enemies who did not acknowledge this nation's God nor this nation's special status before that God.

Another weighty message breathed in from a Catholic grade school atmosphere was that of vocation. A vocation was described as a quiet, gentle, irresistible call by God. The nun teachers told of Ignatius of

Loyola, a Spanish soldier who was wounded in battle and, in the silence and calm of his recovery, heard the call and responded by founding the Jesuits, mighty soldier missionaries for the Lord. St. Stephen, the Church's first martyr, had heard his final call from the lips of the Lord seated on His heavenly throne as Stephen was being stoned to death. St. Paul, who had righteously taken part in Stephen's stoning, did not hear the call to Stephen. Paul's call was neither gentle nor resistible. God wanted him so much that He knocked him out of his saddle and blinded him, until stumbling and groping, Paul begged for baptism and started down the road designated by God. St. Joan of Arc had followed disembodied voices that told her to lead the army of France against the English and to die, burned as a witch. Five hundred years later and four hundred years after the English turned their backs on Rome while the French remained faithful, St. Joan's call was authenticated by the Pope who canonized her.

The call came to each in its own way. Those who deliberately resisted the call spent the remainder of their earthly lives in misery because they were not doing the work that God had from all eternity decreed for them, and, after death, they were denied a place in heaven because they had refused to respond unswervingly, as had the martyr heroes of the early church.

Girls who refused the call to become sisters married cruel and drunken husbands, were poor, had deformed babies, became alcoholics, even prostitutes, suffered sickness, and, when they died, went to a special hell. Boys could look forward to similar kinds of treatment.

For more than two years I had been wrestling with the question of whether I had a call. I envied Old Testament Jacob who had fought with his angel one night and won. His fight was quick and done. His leg was withered in the battle, but he had a sure and unequivocal answer. Life was simpler in those days when God spoke directly to His people. Most of my Catholic school classmates had determined between the ages of eleven and thirteen, when their hormones kicked in, that they definitely were not called to a life of celibacy. In fact, they would resist such a fate with every ounce of will, strength, and devious cunning they were capable of. The nuns stated that such an attitude was a sure sign that they had not received a call. The few of us who had not given in to our chemistry were still trying to determine whether we were or were not among the chosen.

In the face of such a weighty decision, the temptation was to lapse into inertia, to decide by not deciding and so let some extraneous chance factor make the determination. Later, several of my classmates would choose marriage partners on the basis of a chance pregnancy or on the basis of proximity when the pool of eligible partners was perceived as drying up. Choosing one's fate, under those circumstances, was like shopping for a used car.

I would have let the decision wait, but time was moving to a martial beat. The draft was waiting at the end of high school. Further, the school I attended taught Latin only two years. If I waited until my graduation to try my vocation, I would be years behind my peers in the pursuit of my vocation while I made up those neglected studies.

The wooden kneeler made my knees hurt, but there was no other proper posture for struggling with myself over the idea of God's special call. Later, in speaking with other troubled souls, I would hear of God delivering calls late in the evening in bus terminals, in hospitals, in locker rooms, in parking lots outside bars, in whore houses, in the shouts of preachers in tents and on television. But for me, then, the place I expected to hear a message from God was inside that one dim church with its cave-like grottoes, with the four evangelists painted on the ceiling, with its pump organ in the choir loft, and with its plaster statues on pedestals with rows of candles burning before them releasing their smoke into the air like the souls of the dead freed from purgatory by the prayers and offerings of the faithful. Those candles, indeed, burned to force the omnipotent God to exercise His mercy in behalf of relatives and friends who had finished this gravity bound part of their journey. Candles were symbols of the powerful, the good, and the holy, so that they were themselves powerful, good and holy.

Foremost on the positive side of the problem of an ecclesiastical vocation was the understanding that the Catholic priesthood was the source of the highest possible help for mankind. The priest could forgive sins and, thus, ensure that a fellow human's life had not been wasted and that the future for one forgiven as he or she breathed his or her last would be eternal happiness. Even more powerfully, the priest could also reach beyond the grave to release the already dead from purgatory, and here, on this side of the grave, the priest had the arguments to convince the damned to change their lives and the power to exorcise the devil. This was greater power than any politician might have. It was a greater healing work than any physician might undertake.

This work, however, demanded a price. That price was giving up the companionship of a wife, and the satisfaction of one's own children, and the joys of sex. In nineteen forty-seven, I thought that was a fair price, but, because of my lack of experience, I could not but doubt whether I would be able to make and keep that unconditional promise of celibacy.

I went over these considerations several times and spoke to my Lord with "Thee's" and "Thou's," not presuming upon any familiarity that may have developed over my few years of intimacy as an altar boy with the divinity. The divinity reciprocally respected that desire for formality. He offered no clear insight that would allow me to say, "Yes, that is the way it all should be."

The battle continued for some time with no victory. There were considerations brought forward by pride that priests were among the special, the chosen few. Humility, on the other hand, forced the recognition that this was pride speaking and that pride was a sin that had to be excluded from my motivation if I should choose the priesthood, for doing the right thing for the wrong reason invalidated the right thing, no matter how right or how difficult that thing might be.

Presumption, another sin, was also recognized as the possible source of the desire for some heavenly sign. Despair was the mother of the thought that there would never be any solution and that I would discover what my fate should have been only upon facing my Judge after dying.

In my desperate casting about, I focused on the red light suspended in the air above the sanctuary. Ordinarily, it hung from its long chain without motion. On this afternoon it was moving gently, slowly, solemnly, from side to side. This distraction from my internal battle was like coming up from a long, deep dive in a dark and murky river. I had my sign.

I determined that I was to act as though I had a call to the priesthood, and let the future take care of itself. I went to the seminary and spent the next ten years working and praying, studying philosophy and theology, to become a priest. During those years of study, most of the superstitions that my journey had begun with were destroyed, and even the sign of the swaying candle was reduced to a silly accident. The candle had probably been changed earlier in the day and was merely responding to the law of gravity as must any pendulum. The effort of my theological studies was to define the limits of faith and reason and explain what could be explained and bow humbly before those things that could be verified but could not be explained. The swaying candle that I had seen as a direct sign from God could be explained.

    Ten years after that afternoon session in the parish church, I was ordained a Catholic priest in that same church. When the ceremony was over, the Monsignor who had taken the old pastor's place called the new little sister sacristan to him and scolded her for not replacing the candle in the red sanctuary light before the ceremony had started. He was disturbed because the light had flickered and died at the crucial part of the ceremony when the bishop was placing his ordaining hands upon my head.

*

*David Norris*
*Seoul, Korea*

## THIS IS PARADISE

Where is here?
I don't know
where is here
I think here
Is paradise I
Think I want
To die you
Know my feel
He did not
Understand me
He only thinks
Of his own

Sometimes I turn
On the red
Light and I
Think of you
I think it
Must be paradise

*David Norris*
*continued*

She leans back
In the tub
The steam rising
Around her beads
Of sweat scented
Blue water she
Straightens up for
A while and
Then just goes
All to hell

Her face
At times like this
when she is sober
And young and beautiful
I can almost forget
Her indiscretions her midnight
Raving maniac drunk and lost
Telephone pleas for help
The strange men who
Know her who speak
to her on the streets
The bruises on her
Thighs when she
Is like this
Here with me
In paradise

Did you miss me?

Yes.

Me too.

Smiles.

**Dan River Anthology '95//75**

*James Rossignol*
*San Antonio, TX*

## THE SIMPLE ONES PLOD

the simple ones plod
plod past
the mine fields
past the voting booths
the pulpits
the confessionals
the academies
never stopping
not even for
fortified cereal
preferring instead to glut
themselves on knowing
that their plodding affords
even more comfortable shoes
for their children
so their children can keep on plodding
with somewhat less discomfort
the complicated ones study the plodding
not as one would a sacred text
or the entrails of a bird
the moving stars
rather as one would some controlled
experiment whose findings will yield
absolutely nothing of any significance
or the eyes of a victim
the stock market pages
some might even sigh
and write poetry about them
take their folklore to make it
as complicated as art or subject

**(more)**

it to some dissertation
but the simple just plod
that's all
plod past the surveys they're asked to fill out
past the pressure to commit
to a brand
to a party
to a boss
to whichever army
sends them through no man's land
where they'll plod and survive just
like elder statesmen suffering from weak hearts
who fuck much too young whores
daylights out.

*

*Sy Hakim*
*Philadelphia, PA*

## WAITING, BEYOND THE STONE: THE LOSS...

Waiting
behind the stone
beyond
the waves' rise;
will the ghosts return?
Night crowed against day,
the compromises of blue and red
and grey resolves in shades
drawn to, down to
the green of water,
the tiger eyeless flecks of foam:
there is too little—
no reflection to the day.

(more)

In the sky
an absence of shadow, or rise
of cloud, of spirit of self.
Beyond the piled stones
waiting
a sub-way hollow of I
reminiscent, and another time.
Where there should be
a crest to wave,
a sine-form connection
of past to now—
the Benediction,
the delivery that confirms
self to self—
stones wait.
Severed
severe, the silence of the synapse,
the loss of the subtle spark,
the sub-way,
the absence of a voice
and the muse and motion.
Shadow cursed and crushed
beneath the stone
beyond the reach
of the waves' demise,
dim remnant of self
I
still waiting
behind the stone
for the ghost,
merely, the problematic,
the return,
stare.

*Ryan McLaughlin*
*San Francisco, CA*

# FLITTERING

The naked pressure of sickness
builds stone walls from gravel
And crushes faint hearts in loneliness,
bewilderedly feverish in a damp,
stuffy room with a view of a
million lights in a tower,
reaching like teeth for some unreachable
distant and vague knowledge
or placidity.
And the million lights won't stop flittering,
until the naked head is shrinking
into some cubists playground
with wires running around and over everything.
The lights remain etched on blue retinas,
shining light, blindingly, foolishly into dark
cool places where no light is the best policy.
Dark, cool places that we are always the last to see
and always the most surprised.
Dark, cool paces where fevered heat is the only force that
may drive us there, and always seems to keep us there longer
than is required.
Underneath heaps of strawlike blankets,
head rested on a stack of pillows like well-painted stones,
bedside scattered with litter of books half-read and less
comprehended, tissues half-used — as if the short blue carpet
was some operating room floor, and we wait impatiently for some
dark nurse to come and remove the bloody rags before the patient
wakes to find what went on while he was under.
In the half-wakening, sickening, influx of sanity, we
realize the depth and breadth that this little bout with
death's archangels has meant,
we scream (or wish our coughing lungs would bear the breath to):
"Enough is enough! Let me be or simply kill me!"

**Dan River Anthology '95//79**

*Richard Alan Bunch*
*Alameda, CA*

## SONOMA MOUNTAIN

Lying on the couch barely
conscious, my memories
slip and keep slipping
back to the top of
Sonoma Mountain.

What innocence!
Like shooting metaphors!
Picking wildflowers
firm in their yellowy wisdoms.
Clutching them
with such runaway
tenderness
as though we could
undo dying and death.

And your hushed eyes
in their philosophic bones,
kept asking, borne
with a kind of rage and
outstretched wonder,
how many springtimes
you had left.

Until we wound
back down the trail
and mingled with those
maybes once again,
no answer rose.

*Richard Alan Bunch*
*continued*

A ranger said we could
not take the flowers home.
So we tossed them like chips
high into the flames
and higher into the riddles
of this twilight.

*

*Randall Brock*
*Spokane, WA*

## POEM

Silken
air
of dream
in vision
silent
in dance

*

## POEM

lost
rhythm
running
deep
in release
in hands
of speech

*Dr. Doris M. Carter*
*Worcester, MA*

## THE OLD WHEELBARROW

On the snowed-lawn next door
a rotting away wooden wheelbarrow
hugs the snow for dear life.
The blue wheel freezes in thick ice.
The handles, no longer used
spread apart
croaking
under the weight
of heavy sod once holding cheerful flowers
now bedraggled with snarling weeds.

It sits there yelling out its history
of the man who built it years ago
now in a nursing home.
Fell down the stairs and bashed in his head.
He doesn't remember his wheelbarrel.

His daughter planted the geraniums years ago.
Six months later
Dead from cancer of the uterus.

The mother, too old to tend the wheelbarrow,
Too feeble in age to care.
So, the wheelbarrow sits all day
hiding its own story
as it rots away.

*Christine Swanberg*
*Rockford, IL*

# FORT ZACHARY BEACH, KEY WEST

It's a place we return each January
(the cruelest of months)
not for its vast Floridian beaches
laden with oiled beauties
or fine pink sand
but for its gentle slopes,
its cove of slender pines,
the mingling salt waters
of the Gulf and the Atlantic,
the nudge of Cuba 90 miles away.

The wind was brisk but nothing like
the chill we thought we left behind.
The sky was Key West bright
and white sails fluttered
just a stone's throw away, when
a young man walked by, specter-thin
and yellow-skinned, his head bound
by a white scarf that caught my eye
like a gull's wing on the updraft.
He looked like a refugee.

He was like Lawrence of Arabia—
poor soldier of misfortune!
He was like a nun martyred for love.
We wanted him to walk on water.
We wanted him to sail on home.

**Dan River Anthology '95//83**

*Ginni Noonan*
*Reston, VA*

## SOFT TOUCH

You have such a soft touch.
Gentle, like velvet, or satin.
Silk has nothing on it.
It's like a cozy old blanket,
comforting and warm.

You have such a soft touch.
It's like the fur
of a beady-eyed rat, or moss
on the rock that I'll need
as a foothold.

You have such a soft touch.
It's like the skin of a clean,
unbruised apple, only
there's a worm in it,
and I'm starving.

You have such a soft touch.
It's like the delicate stroking
of your fingertips down, down,
down the chalkboard,
which happens to be above an amplifier.

You have such a soft touch.
It's familiar,
as if I've known it forever.
I guess it's because all this time
that I've been writing,
I felt my own touch,
imagining that it was yours.

*L.K. Hoffman*
*Arrow Rock, MO*

## LISTENING THROUGH THE WALL

There must have been a swooshing of sheets
sometime, but
I never interrupted them;
no startled breasts.
Their room was next to mine;
their wall, my wall.
No whisperings,
the bed never crashed,
no thudding, no little shrieks,
no gasping for air like
children learning to float.

I slept tight as I could.
Both arms pressed close,
flat, no pillow, stoic.
Sometimes I'd press two fingers
on my lips hard.
That's all, just the kiss.
I'd study them to see
what love looked like:
in the hall, a passionless kiss.
Once or twice
I practiced on father.

*

## BOYS

The eraser pink balls were
the best for bouncing
and also for making bosoms, (at eleven).

**Dan River Anthology '95//85**

**L.K. Hoffman**
*continued*

A scarf with a rubberband
makes a very good ponytail.

So dressed: I'd go outside
with Kathy to find boys.
She'd flirt. I'd fight,
my form of flirting.

Bobby Lane's father called
mine about his bloody nose
pink bosoms and all.
I didn't know why I'd hit him exactly.

I wonder now
how backwards I still am at making
this connection
and what disasters lie in wait
before I
in some incredible get-up
finally get it right.

*

## FISHING FOR CRAPPIE

We sneak to the dock
in the dark to steal fish.

I pour the coffee.
You roll stink bait to balls.
My son places the poles.

I settle and watch.
You are meticulous, methodical.
You teach my son how it's done.
He's nine,
he doesn't listen hard.
He just wants to fish.

The sky begins to pale
from black to dawn.
I fuss with my paints,
mostly I'm in the way.

The sun creases the wrinkled lake;
copper scribbles from dock to shore.

We speak quietly, as if
we could be overheard, or
were talking intimately;
private lusty subjects, not
"pass the minnows".

We are like those old musty couples
who don't talk, in restaurants,
on buses, they stare past each other
and move in unison, soundlessly
as if they might startle each other

You curse politely.
You were fishing for crappie
and catfish at once.
The cat got breakfast and got away.

**Dan River Anthology '95//87**